Pam Wedgwood's
RecorderWorld

Very first adventures in recorder playing

by PAM WEDGWOOD

illustrations by DREW HILLIER

www.recorderworld.co.uk

Music notation is given in both
English and American terminology throughout

CD notes: some shorter pieces are combined on one track
All concert pieces have rehearsal and performance tempo tracks

© 2003 by Faber Music Ltd
First published in 2003 by Faber Music Ltd
Bloomsbury House 74–77 Great Russell Street London WC1B 3DA
Cover design by Shireen Nathoo Design
Music processed by MusicSet 2000
Printed in England by Caligraving Ltd
All rights reserved

ISBN10: 0-571-51985-7
EAN13: 978-0-571-51985-9

To buy Faber Music publications or to find out about the full range of titles
available please contact your local music retailer or Faber Music sales enquiries:

Faber Music Limited, Burnt Mill, Elizabeth Way, Harlow, CM20 2HX England
Tel: +44 (0)1279 82 89 82   Fax: +44 (0)1279 82 89 83
sales@fabermusic.com   fabermusic.com

This book belongs to

_____

FABER *ff* MUSIC

Doodling!

Are you ready to go on an exciting adventure in RecorderWorld?

①

Out loud, say
DOO, DOO, DOO

Take the head joint off your recorder and hold it in your **LEFT** hand. Now blow into the head joint, making the same 'DOO' shape with your tongue (without saying the word out loud!). Don't blow too hard …

②

Try playing a long
DOOOOOOOOOOOO
and a short DO

Experiment with loud and quiet 'DOO's. Can you hear you are making up a pattern in sound? In music, this is called a rhythm.

③

Ask a partner or your teacher to play a short DOO rhythm on their head joint

Can you play it back to them, like an echo?

④

Now try The Name Game!

✦ Can you work out the rhythm of your name?

✦ Say it first, then 'DOO' it:
Mat-thew = DOO DOO

✦ How many 'DOOS' are there in your name?

✦ Who can 'DOO' your teacher's name?

✦ Who has the most 'DOOS' in their name?

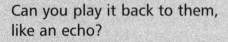

⑤ Now put your recorder together

Put your **RIGHT** thumb underneath the fourth hole.

You should be able to hold your recorder just by resting it on your **RIGHT** thumb and bottom lip – no other fingers.

⑥ The note  B

Cover the thumb hole on the back of your recorder with your **LEFT** thumb and put the first finger of your **LEFT** hand on the first finger hole. Only use the pad of your finger.

This is the note B.

TOP TIP

To remember which hand is which, hold your hands like this and your **LEFT** hand will make an L shape:

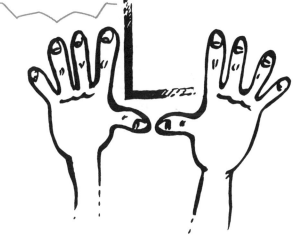

⑦ DOO some more

'DOO' some more rhythm echoes with a partner, on the note B.

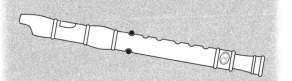

⑧ The ten second challenge

10   9   8   7   6 ...

✧ Start with your recorder on your lap.

✧ Close your eyes.

✧ As your teacher counts down from 10 to 1, see if you can pick up your recorder, put your fingers in position and get ready to play.

STAGE 2

Meet the beats

1 2 3 4

𝅝 = 4 beats
Semibreve/
Whole note

1 2 1 2

𝅗𝅥 = 2 beats
Minim/
Half note

1 1

♩ = 1 beat
Crotchet/
Quarter note

TOP TIP

Put your hand on your heart. Can you feel it beating steadily? In *RecorderWorld*, music has a steady beat or **PULSE** too.

In two groups, one claps the pulse '1 2 3 4' while the other claps the rhythms opposite.

FACT FILE

A **NOTE** is made up of **BEATS**, telling you whether the note is long or short.

•Rhythm box•

SAY, CLAP, then **PLAY** (on the note B)

1 2 3 4 1 2 3 4

I   like   fish and chips

1 2 3 4 1 2 3 4

Jack and Gill went up the hill

1 2 3 4 1 2 3 4

Man-ches-ter U - ni - ted

4

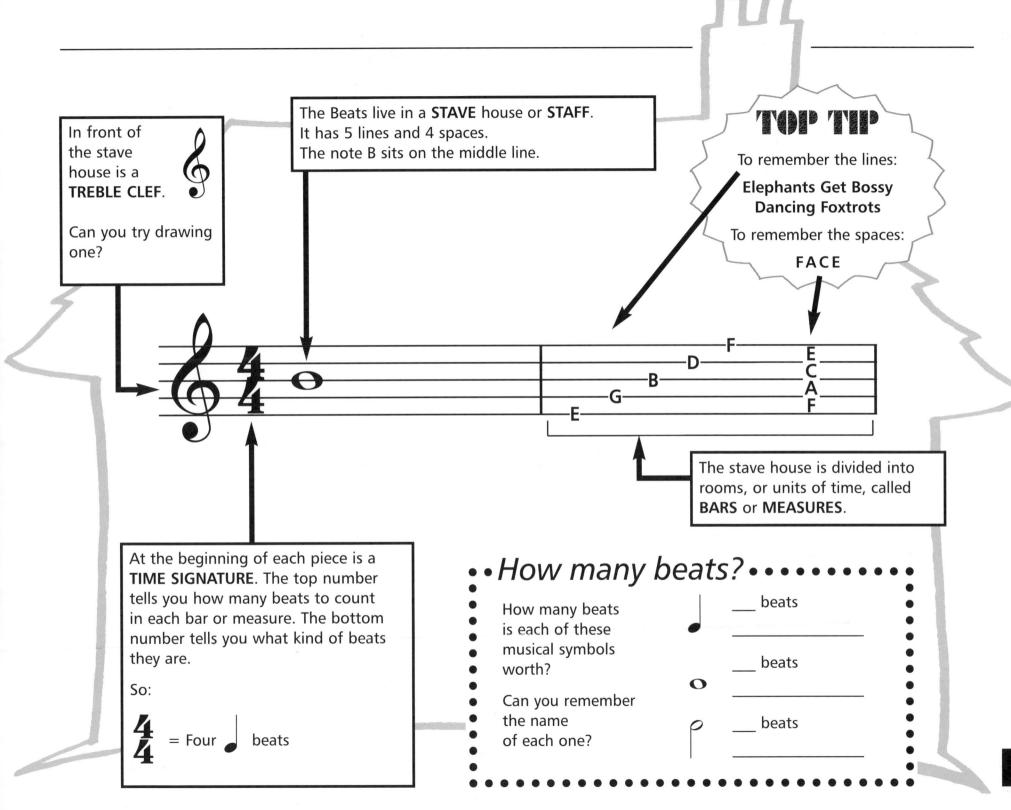

In front of the stave house is a **TREBLE CLEF**.

Can you try drawing one?

The Beats live in a **STAVE** house or **STAFF**.
It has 5 lines and 4 spaces.
The note B sits on the middle line.

TOP TIP

To remember the lines:

Elephants Get Bossy Dancing Foxtrots

To remember the spaces:

F A C E

The stave house is divided into rooms, or units of time, called **BARS** or **MEASURES**.

At the beginning of each piece is a **TIME SIGNATURE**. The top number tells you how many beats to count in each bar or measure. The bottom number tells you what kind of beats they are.

So:

4/4 = Four ♩ beats

How many beats?

How many beats is each of these musical symbols worth?

Can you remember the name of each one?

♩ ___ beats
_____

𝅝 ___ beats
_____

𝅗𝅥 ___ beats
_____

5

Playing B on the stave

TOP TIP

Count 1 2 3 4 before
you come in. If you are
playing along with the CD,
listen for one bar/measure
of clicks so you know
when to start.

PLAYING SKILLS
Can you play this shape?

Now hold the note steady!

Practise yawning, making
sure your shoulders stay
DOWN.

Clap then play

Swinging B

Twinkle, twinkle little star

Twin - kle,   twin - kle   lit - tle   star,

how   I   won - der   what   you   are.

6

New note A

A and B are a **TONE** or **WHOLE STEP** apart. Which sounds higher?

Clap then play

Baa, baa black sheep

Traditional

Baa, baa black sheep, have you a - ny wool?

Yes sir, yes sir, three bags full.

FINGER CRUNCHER

Practise this lots of times to get your fingers going!

Old Macdonald had a farm

Traditional

Old Mac - do - nald had a farm, e - i - e - i - o!

Polly put the kettle on

Traditional

Pol - ly put the ket - tle on, Pol - ly put the ket - tle on,

Pol - ly put the ket - tle on, we'll all have tea.

TRUE or FALSE?

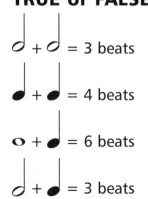

𝅗𝅥 + 𝅗𝅥 = 3 beats

♩ + ♩ = 4 beats

𝅝 + ♩ = 6 beats

𝅗𝅥 + ♩ = 3 beats

7

Concert time

Russian dance

Lively

Creepy crawlies

Creepily

Na - sty, hai - ry, cree - py craw - lies,

crawl a - long the bed - room floor at night!

Lazy cowboy blues

Lazily

17.9.13

FACT FILE

Music can sound happy and sad.

Music that sounds happy is usually in a **MAJOR** key. Music that sounds sad is usually in a **MINOR** key.

Listen to the accompaniments. Can you tell which pieces on this page are major, and which are minor?†

TOP TIP

Did you all finish together?

Make sure you hold the last note for its full value, then come off.

𝅝

1 2 3 4 STOP!

† Russian dance – minor. Creepy crawlies – minor. Lazy cowboy blues – major.

8

New note G

Jingle bells

James Pierpont

You'll be able to play the rest of this tune when you reach page 26

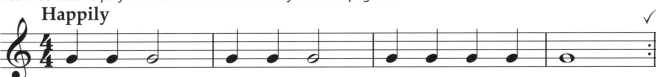

Happily

Jin-gle bells,   jin-gle bells,   jin-gle all the way.

I like holidays

Longingly

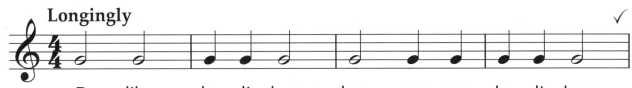

I   like   ho - li - days,   long   sum - mer   ho - li - days.

I   like   ho - li - days,   play - ing   in   the   sun.

Dreaming

✓10/13

In a daze

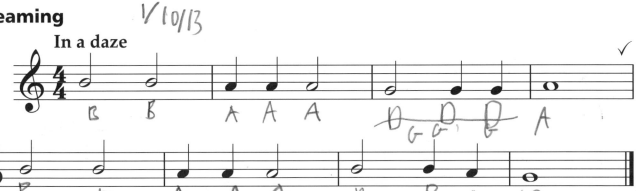

FINGER CRUNCHER

24.9.13

B G B A B

BAG challenge

Close your eyes and ask someone to say one of the new notes you have learnt: **B A** or **G**.

How long does it take you to find the fingering and play the note?

Who can do it the fastest? Have a competition with your friends!

A mixed bag

CONGRATULATIONS –

*now you can play three notes on the recorder; B, A and G.
Can you tell which is the highest note? And the lowest?*

PLAYING SKILLS

If your recorder sounds blocked up, give it a quick suck. It won't get blocked up as often if you warm it up on your sleeve or under your arm before you play it.

All mixed up

 PIANO ACCOMPANIMENT

Mystery tunes

Can you tell which two tunes make up this duet?†

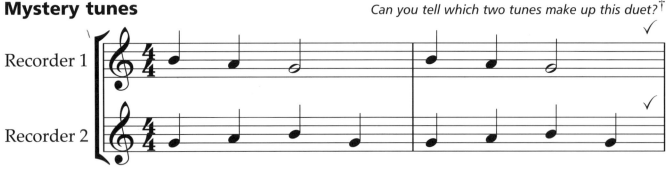

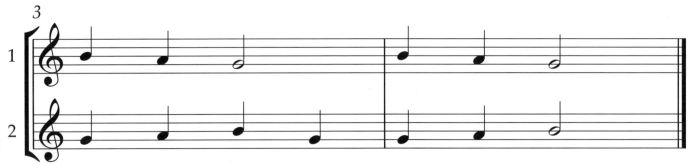

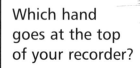

QUICK QUIZ

Which hand goes at the top of your recorder?

Which fingers do we use for the note G?

Explain how to tongue a note

Which fingers do we use for A?

Clap and say a word rhythm (see page 4 if you're stuck!)

† *Frère Jacques and Three Blind Mice*

Concert time

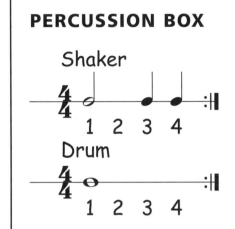

PERCUSSION BOX

Shaker

1 2 3 4

Drum

1 2 3 4

TOP TIP

Try to breathe only where you see a

✓

LOST LETTERS

Find the missing letter to complete each word below. Their clues are the notes next to each one.

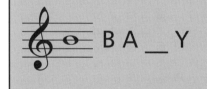

B A _ Y

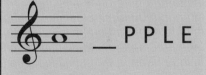

_ P P L E

R U _

Suo-gân

Welsh traditional

PIANO ACCOMPANIMENT

g A B A g A

3

g A B A B g

3-note samba

PIANO ACCOMPANIMENT

Samba-style

5

2/4 time signature

FACT FILE

The time signature 2/4 tells you to count

two ♩ beats

in each bar/measure.

Mighty mouse march

16
PIANO ACCOMPANIMENT

March time

Ragamuffin

17
PIANO ACCOMPANIMENT

Rag time

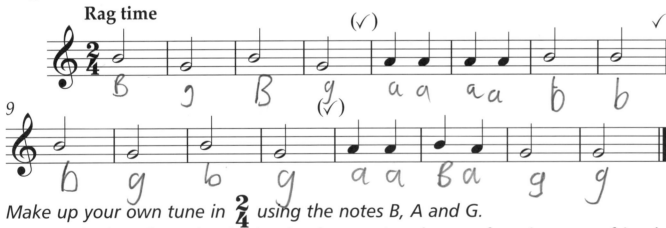

Make up your own tune in 2/4 using the notes B, A and G.
Choose rhythms from the rhythm bank opposite, then perform it to your friends!

TOP TIP

In 2/4, listen for two bars/measures of clicks on the CD before you start.

RHYTHM BANK

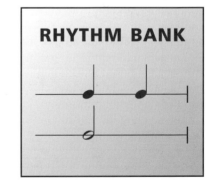

Concert time

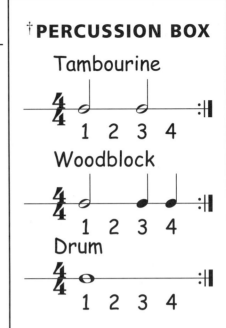

Stand to attention†

Proudly

At ease

Relaxed

B g a B B g a g g

Quick march

Briskly

B B B g A A B

B B B g A B G

Robin's rock

Rock 'n' roll

B B G A B   B B G A B

G G G   G G G.   B B B A G

A A A   G G G   B B B A G

---

†PERCUSSION BOX

Tambourine

4/4   1 2 3 4

Woodblock

4/4   1 2 3 4

Drum

4/4   1 2 3 4

PLAYING SKILLS

Without puffing your cheeks out, blow as if you were blowing up a balloon. Notice how steady and even your breathing is? Remember this when you play the tunes on this page.

TOP TIP

Have a look at your **RIGHT** hand. Make sure your fingers are still in the correct position, next to the holes. (See page 3 for a reminder!)

Have a rest

FACT FILE

A rest is a silent space in the music.

Each note has its own special rest shape.

1-beat rest
crotchet rest/ = 𝄽
quarter rest

Clap each part separately first.

Fiddlesticks

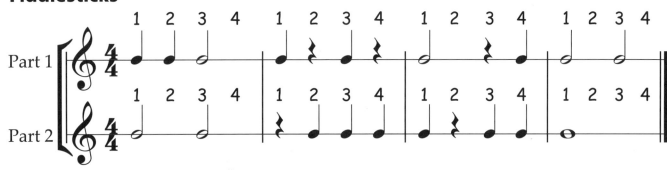

Chopsticks

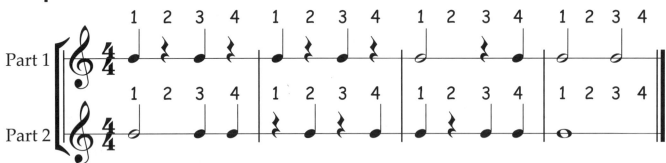

TOP TIP

Make up an action to do in each rest.

A sniff, a hand sign, or even a toe curl will help at first!

Now try writing your own rhythm using ♩ ♪ 𝅝 and 𝄽 – make sure there are four beats in each bar/measure. With a partner, each clap your piece and you've made a duet!

Concert time

A restful day †

Peacefully

26 27 PIANO ACCOMPANIMENT

The Train †

The whistle's blowing!

28 29 PIANO ACCOMPANIMENT

slowing down

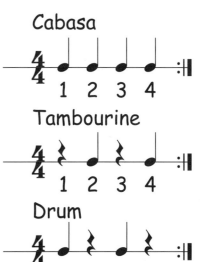

Cabasa
4/4 1 2 3 4

Tambourine
4/4 1 2 3 4

Drum
4/4 1 2 3 4

FACT FILE

— 2-beat rest
■ minim rest/ half rest

WHISTLE
LIKE A TRAIN

Finger any note on your recorder, then partially cover and uncover the sound hole on your mouthpiece with the other hand to make a train's whistle! What other sound effects can you play on your recorder?

START HERE

Choose a start position and try to get to the middle of the maze as quickly as you can, doing as many of the quick quizzes as possible along the way.

You can play this game on your own or, by taking one position each, race against a friend!

FINISH

Go back and play **Robin's rock**

Go back and play **Ragamuffin**

Play a sound effect on your recorder

Work out the rhythm of your surname

Clap the rhythm of **Happy birthday**

Draw a treble clef

Play the lowest note you know on the recorder

How many beats in $\frac{4}{4}$?

TRUE or FALSE

♩ + ♩ = 3 beats

What can you do if your notes sound squeaky?

Go back and play **Creepy crawlies**

Which hand **ALWAYS** goes at the top of your recorder?

THIS WAY ➡

THIS WAY

THAT WAY

Show the correct position of your **RIGHT** hand

Draw a 2-beat note (and its rest)

TRUE or **FALSE** music in a minor key usually sounds sad

What can you do if your recorder sounds blocked up?

STAGE 9

New note C

TOP TIP

Did you spot the new time signature of 3/4? It means count 3 beats in each bar.

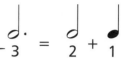

FACT FILE

This is a **DOTTED MINIM** or **DOTTED HALF NOTE**. It lasts for three beats.

When you see a dot after a note or a rest, the dot makes it longer by HALF as much again.

Waltzing around

FINGER CRUNCHER

Swinging C †

Jazzy waltz

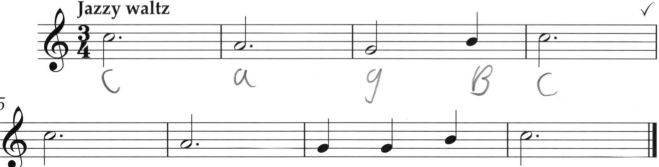

†PERCUSSION BOX

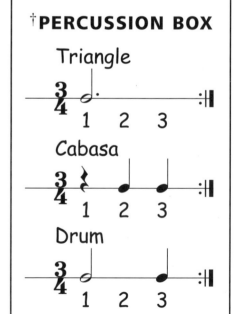

Triangle

Cabasa

Drum

18

Quavers/eighth notes

Clap, say, then play each part separately first. Then get into four groups and play all four parts together. Repeat as many times as you like!

Food fest!

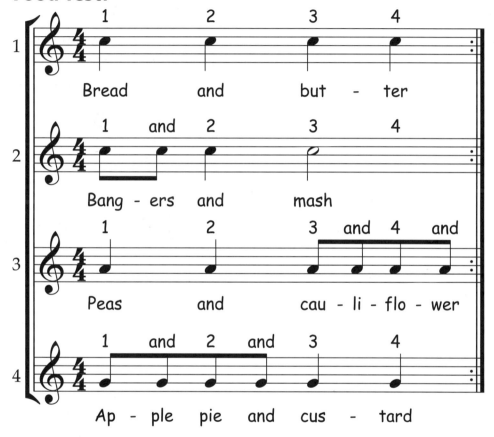

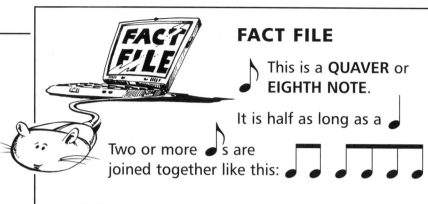

FACT FILE

♪ This is a **QUAVER** or **EIGHTH NOTE**.

It is half as long as a ♩

Two or more ♪s are joined together like this: ♫ ♫♫

A whole bar/measure rest (in any time signature) looks like this: ▬

Follow my leader

TOP TIP

Count 'and' for the second ♪ of each beat.

1 and 2 and

Slurs

FACT FILE

This is a slur:

⌒ or ⌣

A slur joins **DIFFERENT** notes together, telling you to play them smoothly.

Tongue only the first note – join the other notes together in one long breath.

Two's company

Rattle snake round

A round is a piece in which several players have the same music, but start one after the other. Group 2 start when Group 1 get to figure ⟨2⟩.

PLAYING SKILLS

Tear a long, thin strip of newspaper. Hold it 15cm away from your nose and blow. See how long you can hold the paper horizontal with your breath! (If you feel dizzy: **STOP!**)

Count 1 2 3   **Carefully!**

I slither here, I slither there, I slide round with-out a care. My poi-s'nous bite will make you ill; if you see me stand quite still!

20

Concert time

In the 'O' zone

Respectfully

PIANO COMPANIMENT

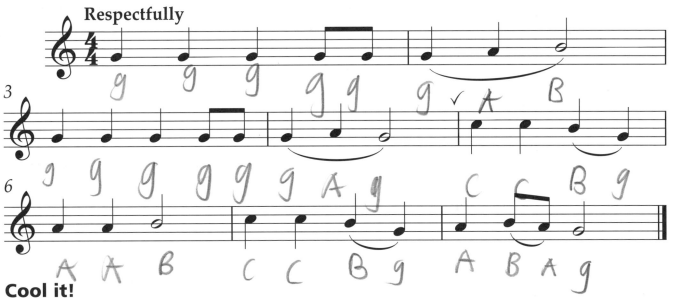

PERCUSSION BOX

Cymbal

4/4

1 2 3 4

Woodblock

4/4

1 2 3 4

Drum

4/4

1 2 3 4

Cool it!

With a bossa nova feel

PIANO COMPANIMENT

When the sun is ve - ry hot,

wear hats and sun - cream quite a lot!

BOSSA NOVA!

Bossa nova is a type of music that comes from Brazil. It is very rhythmic and good for dancing to!

21

Dynamics

Minuet for two mice

FACT FILE

p is short for *piano*, which means play quietly.

f is short for *forte*, which means play loudly (but don't force the sound).

p and *f* are **DYNAMICS**.

Try playing the whole piece through once loudly, once quietly, then with the dynamics marked.

Which do you prefer? Why?

Think about other loud and quiet sounds. Make a list of each:

LOUD

an alarm clock
_____
_____

QUIET

a whisper
_____
_____

Old Macdonald's jambouree

* Make up an animal to go here …
? And an animal sound to go here!

Old Mac-do-nald had a farm, e - i - e - i - o. And
on that farm he had some * e - i - e - i - o. With a
? ? here, ? ? there, here a ? there a ? ev-'ry-where a ? ?
Old Mac-do-nald had a farm, e - i - e - i - o.

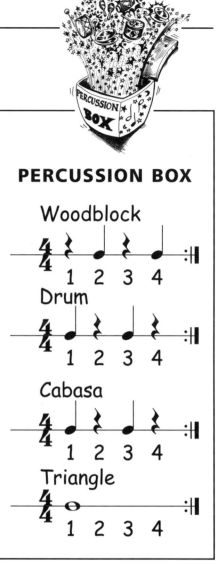

PERCUSSION BOX

Woodblock

Drum

Cabasa

Triangle

23

New note D

STAGE 13

PLAYING SKILLS

A dot above or below a note means play it **STACCATO**, or very short. Use a 'tut, tut' shape with your tongue, leaving a space between each note.

The opposite to staccato is **LEGATO**, which means play very smoothly.

TOP TIP

When playing staccato notes, **NEVER** force the sound!

Stegosaurus stomp

PERCUSSION BOX

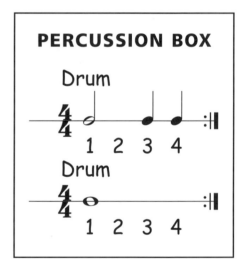

Can you make up your own dinosaur piece?

Remember to give it a title.

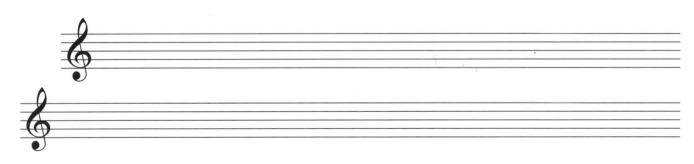

FINGER CRUNCHER

24

Concert time

Dance of the Diplodocus

With a good plod!

CLAP AND COUNT

FACT FILE

A curved line joining two of the **SAME** notes is called a tie. Don't tongue the second one – just count it.

It should sound like one long note.

Lazy Tyrannosaurus

Slowly

1st and 2nd time bars

FACT FILE

The first time through, play the **1ST TIME BAR**: then repeat from the beginning. The next time through, miss out the 1st time bar. Go to the **2ND TIME BAR** instead and play to the end of the piece.

Jingle bells

Dangerous waters

PERCUSSION BOX

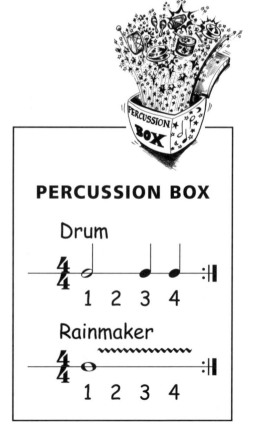

26

Sonata

Wolfgang Amadeus Mozart

Surprise symphony

Franz Joseph Haydn

44 PIANO COMPANIMENT

CLASSICAL **MUSIC**

The music on this page is called classical music.

Mozart and Haydn are very famous classical composers. What else can you find out about them? Ask your teacher to play you some of their orchestral music.

PERCUSSION BOX
bar 16

Drum

Cymbal

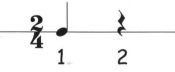

New note E

Now it's time to put your RIGHT hand into action!

Ambulance siren

FINGER CRUNCHER

On this special day

Let's be hap-py, full of joy, on this spe-cial day. Hap-py in our work and play, on this spe-cial day, to-day!

TOP TIP
Make sure your right-hand thumb is directly underneath the first finger of your right hand.

CLAP AND COUNT

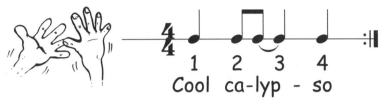

Cool ca-lyp - so

CALYPSO!

Calypso is a type of music that comes from the Caribbean. Like Bossa nova, it is very rhythmic and gets your toes a-tapping …

Cool calypso

PIANO OMPANIMENT

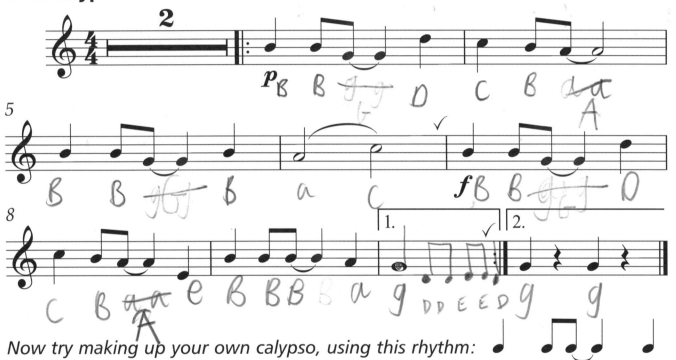

Now try making up your own calypso, using this rhythm:

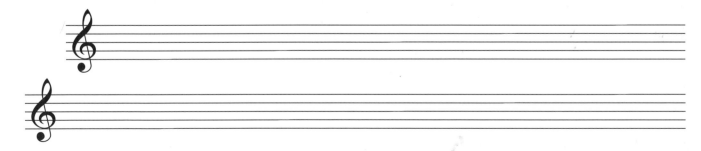

PERCUSSION BOX

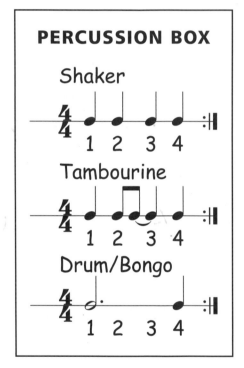

Shaker

Tambourine

Drum/Bongo

Around the recorder world

Can you guess which country each of these pieces describes?

Ellie the elephant

PERCUSSION BOX

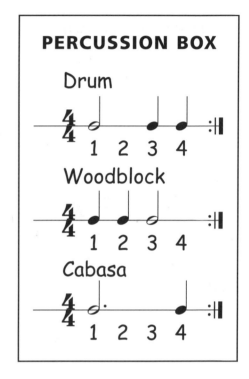

Will it ever rain?

PERCUSSION BOX

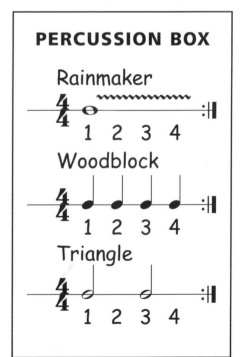

Out on the range

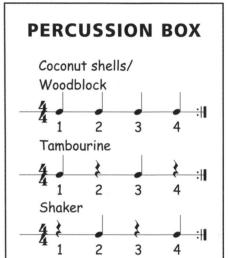

PERCUSSION BOX

Coconut shells/
Woodblock

Tambourine

Shaker

Spicy noodlin'

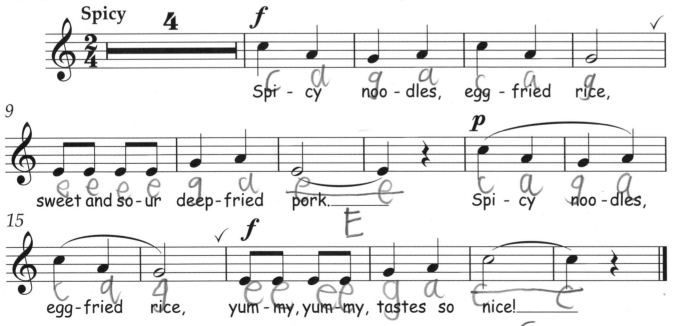

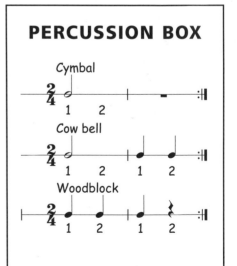

PERCUSSION BOX

Cymbal

Cow bell

Woodblock

3

Certificate

Name
_____

CONGRATULATIONS!

You are now halfway through your adventures in **RecorderWorld**.

We hope you've enjoyed yourself along the way.
See you in book 2!

*From all your friends in **RecorderWorld***

SIGNED (teacher)
_____

(date) _____

Here are all the notes you have learnt so far:

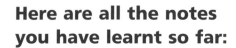

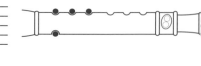

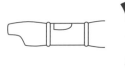